PUPPET PLAY

The Three Little Pigs

Moira Butterfield

Heinemann LIBRARY

First published in Great Britain in 1998 by Heinemann Library,
Halley Court, Jordan Hill, Oxford, OX2 8EJ,
a division of Reed Educational & Professional Publishing Ltd.
Heinemann is a registered trademark of Reed Educational & Professional Publishing Ltd.

OXFORD FLORENCE PRAGUE MADRID ATHENS
MELBOURNE AUCKLAND KUALA LUMPUR SINGAPORE TOKYO
IBADAN NAIROBI KAMPALA JOHANNESBURG GABORONE
PORTSMOUTH NH CHICAGO MEXICO CITY SAO PAULO

Editor: Alyson Jones
Designer: Joanna Hinton-Malivoire
Illustrator: Caroline Jayne Church
Printed and bound in Italy.

02 01 00 99 98
10 9 8 7 6 5 4 3 2 1

British Library Cataloguing in Publication Data
Butterfield, Moira
    Three little pigs - (Puppet play)
    1. Tales - Juvenile drama 2. Children's plays, English
    3. Puppets - Juvenile literature
    I. Title 822.9'14

ISBN 0 431 03478 8 (Hardback)
       0 431 03482 6 (Paperback)

You will need to use scissors and glue to make
the puppets and props for your play. Always
make sure an adult is there to help you.

CONTENTS

THE STORY OF THE THREE LITTLE PIGS

Three little pigs build themselves houses of straw, sticks and bricks. Now you can make puppets to act out their story and see how a job well done saves one of the pigs from a hungry wolf.

READING THE PLAY

There are four puppet characters in this play:

Percy Pig
Impatient

Pete Pig
Patient and careful

Sometimes the **puppeteer** speaks. That's the person who works the puppets.

Polly Pig
Lazy

The Wolf
Mean and hungry

Do this part in an ordinary voice.

If you want to perform this story as a puppet show there are some tips for you on pages 6-9.

If you prefer, ignore the stage directions and read the play with a friend. Share out the parts between you.

The play is split up into parts. Next to each part there is a name so you know who should be speaking.

Percy

I'm Percy Pig and I like to have fun. I don't want to spend all day building a brick house. I'll build my home from straw. That won't take too long.

Sometimes there are stage directions. They are suggestions for things you might get puppets to do at a performance.

Hold up the straw house prop next to Percy.

MAKING PUPPETS

* Card
* Coloured paper
* Paint

* Plant pot sticks
* Scissors
* Pencil

* Grey wool or fake fur
* White paper
* Glue and sticky tape

1 Draw the puppet shapes on card. The sizes here will fit the theatre on page 9. Cut them out.

2 Decorate the shapes with paint and glue on pieces of coloured paper.

3 Tape a stick at the back of the puppet. Use lots of tape so the puppet doesn't fall off.

6

PIG DECORATION

Make three pigs and paint a different t-shirt on each one.

WOLF DECORATION

Stick grey wool or fake fur on the wolf's chest. You could also glue on white paper triangles to give him fierce-looking claws and sharp teeth.

To work a puppet, hold it at the bottom of the stick. Make sure your hand stays hidden.

Making Props

What You Need
* Card
* Paint or coloured paper
* Twigs and straw
* Plant pot sticks
* Scissors and pencil
* Glue and sticky tape

The Fire

1 Cut out a card shape as shown. It is a triangle with a pot and flames on top. Colour the flames red.

2 Collect some twigs and cut them up to make short lengths. Glue them onto the card. Tape a plant pot stick to the back.

Pigs' Houses
Cut out three card houses and tape each one to a plant pot stick.

Straw House
Paint the house to look like yellow straw, or paint it yellow and glue some real straw to it.

Stick House
Paint the house to make it look like sticks, or paint it brown and glue some real twigs on top.

Brick House
Make sure the brick house has a chimney. Paint the house to look as if it is made of bricks.

MAKING A THEATRE

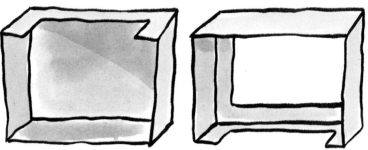

1 Cut the two bumper packets as shown. Tape back any strips that fall off and tape all the joints to make them secure.

WHAT YOU NEED

* Two bumper-sized cereal packets
* Two medium-sized cereal packets
* Coloured paper or paints
* Glue and sticky tape
* Scissors

2 Glue the two together as shown and add some tape too, to make the join really strong. Glue and tape a medium-sized box to each side to help your theatre stand up.

3 Decorate the theatre with coloured paper or paints. Stick extra card shapes on if you like, such as a pointed top.

4 Stand the theatre on a table so you can comfortably hide behind it with your puppets and book. Prop the book inside, or lay it flat on the table. Then practise before you invite an audience to watch your play.

THE THREE LITTLE PIGS

Talk to your audience.

Puppeteer

Hello everyone. I'm here to tell you the story of the three little pigs. They were called Percy, Polly and Pete.

Show the pig puppets one by one.

Puppeteer

One day it was time for them to leave their mother's home and build houses of their own. Let's see what happened.

Duck down and show the audience Percy Pig

Percy Pig

I'm Percy Pig and I like to have fun. I don't want to spend all day building a brick house. I'll build my home from straw. That won't take too long.

Hold up the straw house prop next to Percy.

Show the audience Polly Pig.

I'm Polly Pig and I'm feeling sleepy. I can't be bothered to mess about with bricks.

Polly Pig

Make a yawning noise.

I'll pile up some sticks to build my house. Then I can have a nice long nap.

Polly Pig

Hold up the stick house prop next to Polly. Then take them both down.

12

Show the audience Pete Pig.

> I'm Pete Pig and I know that brick houses are the best. I'll build my house properly.

Pete Pig

Take down Pete Pig. Make some banging noises as if he's busy building (try banging a rolled-up newspaper on the floor). Then show the brick house prop and Pete Pig.

> There. My house is finished.

Pete Pig

In one hand, hold Percy behind the straw house to show that Percy is in his home. Hold the wolf in the other hand. Make some growling and sniffing noises.

Wolf

Grrrr. I'm a hungry wolf who wants some piggy for my breakfast. I can smell one hiding in this straw house.

Move the wolf nearer to Percy's house.

Wolf

Little Pig, little pig, let me come in. Or I'll huff and I'll puff and I'll blow your house in!

Percy

No, wicked wolf. I won't let you in! Not by the hairs on my chinny-chin chin!

Wolf

Then I'll huff and I'll puff and I'll blow your house in!

Make blowing noises. Shake Percy and the house, then drop them and the wolf out of sight.

Percy

Ooh! Help!

15

Hold Polly behind the stick house in one hand, and hold the wolf in the other.

Now I want some piggy for my lunch. I can smell one hiding in this stick house.

Wolf

Move the wolf near to the house. Sniff and make a knocking noise.

Little pig, little pig, let me come in. Or I'll huff and I'll puff and I'll blow your house in!

Wolf

Polly

No, no, wicked wolf. I won't let you in. Not by the hairs on my chinny-chin chin!

Wolf

Then I'll huff and I'll puff and I'll blow your house in!

Make some blowing noises. Shake Polly and the house, then drop them and the wolf out of sight.

Polly

Ooh! Help!

Put up Pete behind the stone house in one hand, and hold the wolf in the other.

I'm still hungry. I want some piggy for my tea. I can smell one hiding in this brick house.

Wolf

Move the wolf closer to the house. Sniff and make a knocking noise.

Little pig, little pig, let me come in. Or I'll huff and I'll puff and I'll blow your house in!

Wolf

Pete

No, no, wicked wolf. I won't let you in! Not by the hairs on my chinny-chin chin!

Wolf

Then I'll huff and I'll puff and I'll blow your house in!

Make lots of blowing noises. Ask the audience to help, if you like.

Wolf

This is harder than I thought. Everybody help me. Blow!

The wolf keeps blowing and panting for a while.

20

Wolf: This won't do. I can't get in. I'll have to think of another way. Let me see ...

Move the wolf near to the house as though he's looking closely at it.

Wolf: ... I know! I'll climb down the chimney.

Take the wolf and the house off so only Pete is on-stage.

Now I'll build a fire and put a pot of hot water on it. Soon the wolf will be in the soup!

Pete

Take Pete off stage. Hold up the fire prop and the wolf.

Move the wolf along the stage towards the fire.

Watch out, porky piggy! I'm coming down the chimney!

Wolf

Put the wolf behind the fire, as if he's jumped into the pot.

Ow! Ow! My fur is frazzled!

Wolf

23

Take the wolf off. Pop your head up
along with Pete Pig. Speak to the audience.

Puppeteer

The wolf's gone away.

Pete

Hurrah!

Puppeteer

Do you think he'll be back?

Wait for the audience
to shout NO!

Puppeteer

And nor will I.
Goodbye!

THE END